THE BEST OF

2013

MATTHEW PRITCHETT

studied at St Martin's School of Art in London and first saw himself published in the *New Statesman* during one of its rare lapses from high seriousness. He has been the *Daily Telegraph*'s front-page pocket cartoonist since 1988. In 1995, 1996, 1999, 2005 and 2009 he was the winner of the Cartoon Arts Trust Award and in 1991, 2004 and 2006 he was 'What the Papers Say' Cartoonist of the Year. In 1996, 1998, 2000, 2008 and 2009 he was the *UK Press Gazette* Cartoonist of the Year and in 2002 he received an MBE.

Own your favourite Matt cartoons. Browse the full range of Matt cartoons and buy online at www.telegraph.co.uk/photographs or call 020 7931 2076.

The Daily Telegraph

THE BEST OF

MATT

2013

An Orion Paperback

First published in Great Britain in 2013 by Orion Books
A division of the Orion Publishing Group Ltd
Orion House
5 Upper Saint Martin's Lane
London, WC2H 9EA

A Hachette UK Company

10 9 8 7 6 5 4 3 2 1

A CIP catalogue record for this book
is available from the British Library.

ISBN: 978 1 4091 2157 2

Printed in the UK by CPI William Clowes, Beccles NR34 7TL

The Orion Publishing Group's policy is to use papers that
are natural, renewable and recyclable products and
made from wood grown in sustainable forests. The logging
and manufacturing processes are expected to conform to
the environmental regulations of the country of origin.

www.orionbooks.co.uk

'I'm on the cheapest
energy tariff – it's called
Being Cut Off'

THE BEST OF
MATT
2013

'You remember you
wanted a pony?'

'What's in this burger?
It just jumped over
my chips'

'I see a lot of travel:
Romania, Luxembourg,
Holland, France, UK ...'

Transportation of meat

'An EU budget is like a Findus lasagne – full of nasty surprises'

Horse meat

Roses are red
Violets are cute
Enjoy your lasagne
Watch out for the 'Bute'

'If you don't hand in your homework it's double school lunch for you'

'You work at the BBC?
So are you a tax dodger or
a paedophile?'

CELEBRITY FALLS FURTHER
THAN ANY OTHER BEFORE

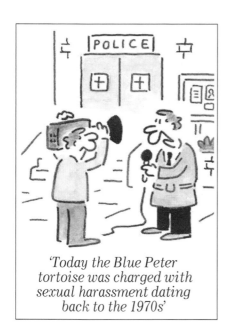

'Today the Blue Peter tortoise was charged with sexual harassment dating back to the 1970s'

'A witch, living in a sweetie house in the forest. Why didn't anyone raise concerns?'

'If I don't renew our TV licence the BBC will name me as a paedophile'

'I don't know what I
pressed, but two more BBC
executives just resigned'

'Hello BBC? I'm about to
switch to another channel.
Do I get a pay-off?'

Problems for Lib Dems

'Asking you to vote
Lib Dem does not count
as an inappropriate suggestion'

Huhne

'I've invented the wheel,
but my wife's going to
take the blame'

'I'm a traditionalist.
I believe that only a man
and a woman should
exchange speeding points'

Huhne

'If I pay my husband's fine
will we both end up in jail?'

'It's a tattoo of a wind
turbine. I shared a cell
with Chris Huhne'

Huhne family texts
become public

'Why couldn't you have flu like everyone else?'

'Their numbers have
to be controlled'

'Is that a ham sandwich?
Will you swap it for
a badger one?'

'I considered becoming a vicar, but the Church's attitude to women is so stuck in the Dark Ages'

'It's terribly sad. He's a
lapsed capitalist'

'Daddy, are old
Etonians everywhere?'

'Step outside and repeat
what you just said about
Lady Thatcher being divisive'

'Have you noticed how much better the weather was back then?'

'It was at the cinema with me that Margaret first used the phrase, No, No, No'

Early life revealed

'Have you seen the
neighbours' new extension?'

'We'll never get home.
Let's bribe a planning official
and build a house right here'

'You've got a huge
wasps' nest and they're
building a 26ft extension'

Royals

'My wife rushes out and buys anything she sees Kate wearing'

Paparazzi photograph Kate topless

Kate dominates the news

'There won't be another
River Pageant, will there?'

'So this Coronation
Chicken must have been
in here for 60 years'

60th anniversary of Queen's Coronation

'I'm in the school play. I'm a shepherd and I marry one of the other shepherds'

'And is that gay mistletoe?'

'Around Christmas I usually decide I'm against marriage between a man and a woman'

'Actually, I've changed my mind. I think I'll marry the best man instead'

'The ayes have it.
You may now kiss the
Deputy Prime Minister'

'Mum, Dad, there's something
I have to tell you. I think
I'm a swivel-eyed loon'

Opponents smeared

Abu Qatada

'You've got radical cleric mice. They're impossible to get rid of'

'In that case, I don't think we should let him go'

'I'm joining a sect which believes the world is going to end on December 21st'

Private depositors bail out bank

'Sorry, doctor, the chef
doesn't work in the evenings'

'The doctor won't come,
so I've ordered a pizza with
penicillin topping'

Out of hours service

NHS Scandals

'They're for Sir David Nichol-son – in case he gets thirsty'

Mid-Staffs scandal

'I hear we've been put on a pathway to shepherd's pie'

'Warning: the following
item contains strong language
right from the start'

'It was snowing when I bought this house. I had no idea it was near Heathrow'

'We're going to the North Pole for Easter, so we'll feel the benefit when we come back'

'If we lash together all
our Christmas trees we
can build a raft'

'The car developed a looser
relationship with the
road and then it decided
to leave altogether'

'My husband uses this to time how long to have the central heating on'

'Can I switch to cheaper wind?'

'The barbecue is now under
No Overall Control'

'My wife thinks Nick Clegg
talks sense. I will be making a
separate statement after hers'

Local election wipeout

Coalition Problems

'It might be nice to let Mr Mitchell leave through the main gate today'

'If I'd wanted to be sneered at, I'd have joined the Conservative party'

Plebgate

Broken promises

Child Care

CHILD CARE PLAN

'A good dog can look after
as many as 30 toddlers'

'It's a picture of my
nursery classroom'

'It's to deter
binge travelling'

'He doesn't play with the
trains, he just puts up
the fares'

'48% of me wants to
stay up, but 49% of me
intends to go to bed'

'We must reach across the
political divide to our
dumb-ass opponents'

(Caption to be supplied by cross-party committee of MPs)

'Sorry about your newspaper. Lord Leveson got to it'

Biting Footballer

'Here at Liverpool it's the second half – or as Luis Suarez calls it, dessert'

'The Lib Dems have proposed a wealth tax on anyone with a full tank of petrol'

'They may look cute,
but they eat all the
green shoots of recovery'

'Recessions are like
Martinis – three is too many'

Fake bomb detectors
produced

'I witnessed the carnage at
Wimbledon, but I'll never
speak about it'

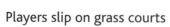

Players slip on grass courts

'Your heart's fine. Just
don't do anything stupid like
watch today's Murray match'

Murray triumphs

'The souvenir tea towels are coming 20 minutes apart'

The world watches and waits

'PUSH ... PUSH!'

'That means Prince George
is in residence'

New Royal Baby visits Middletons

And finally...

'Clown or fruitcake?'

UKIP

'The office called. I've got to go back to work'

'Yes, the earth did move, but that's because they're fracking for gas locally'

'What? NO... Ferguson CAN'T retire!!!'

And finally...

'I know I was hogging the middle lane, but the mobile reception is better there'

'It's a £100 fine for hogging the middle-of-the-road section too long'

New traffic rules

'The winner is the player
with no houses at the
end of the game'

'Question to judge:
what is meant by the term
"Push to Enter"?'

Jury dismissed for asking too
many questions

And finally...

POLICE RECRUITMENT SHAKE-UP

'Our new police chief is some Danish woman'

'I hope details of this incident won't be stored on my microchip'

'Darling, the babysitters
are here'

Fox attacks baby

'The jobless should do what
I do: get out of bed, go to work
and skive there'

And finally...

'My name is Tom and I don't care about the new David Bowie single'

Remains of Richard III found

'That reminds me, it must be
time to bleed the customers'

And finally...

And finally...

'I see you buying the
iPhone 5 and then, shortly
after, Apple launching
the iPhone 6'

'We thought the expansion of
Heathrow was going ahead'

'I dreamt Scotland split from the UK and we got Gordon Brown at weekends'

And finally...

And finally…

Thatcher funeral

'We became suspicious after
one of the Sheikh's horses
won the Tour de France'

'I've been an utter fool.
It's all wrong, you can't have
the West Coast franchise'

And finally...

'I said I'm scared!
I don't want a teddy,
I want a loaded gun'

'For one ghastly moment
I thought they were
building a wind farm'

'Mrs Putin gets the nuclear
missiles at weekends'

The Putins divorce

And finally...

And finally...

'With 10 years of rain forecast, we've developed a potato that can swim'

'They can't build HS2 here if someone discovers a rare species of beetle'

GM crops

'Either your car's chosen
a new Pope, or the exhaust
needs looking at'

'Right, now who are
we backing in the
Cheltenham Gold Cup?'

Pope resigns

And finally...

And finally...

Snooping

'Hello, is that the CIA? Does my family know it's Father's Day?'

'I made them to stop the CIA seeing into our living room'

Snooping

'I filled the duvet
with frozen peas'

'I want to sail somewhere
cold so I can claim my
winter fuel allowance'

And finally...

And finally...

'Wish me luck. This is my chance to get off the bottom of the surgeons' league table'

'Would you mind if some students watched me cover up your botched operation?'

'The surgeon thinks he might
have left his gagging order
inside you'

'Your health is so good,
you could even survive
a brief stay in hospital'

And finally...

'COR! I'd like to give her
diversity training'

Church competes with Wonga

'We can't give you a huge
bonus, but the bank would like
to buy your tie for £3m'

'I have to be very careful
with tax. Too much makes
me feel shaky and panicky'